animals**animals**

Donkeys

by **Darice Bailer**

mc **Marshall Cavendish**
Benchmark
New York

Special thanks to Donald E. Moore III, associate director of animal care at the Smithsonian Institution's National Zoo, for his expert reading of this manuscript

The author would like to thank Lucy Fensom of Safe Haven for Donkeys in the Holy Land for her heart-felt support, generosity, and kindness while preparing this manuscript. The author would also like to express her gratitude to Dr. Fiona Marshall, associate professor of anthropology at Washington University in St. Louis, for offering her findings from years of international research on donkeys in Africa and elsewhere. Finally, thank you to Dr. Patricia D. Moehlman, chair of the International Union for Conservation of Nature/Species Survival Commission, who reviewed parts of this manuscript during her work in Tanzania.

Published by Marshall Cavendish Benchmark
An imprint of Marshall Cavendish Corporation

Other Marshall Cavendish Offices:
Marshall Cavendish International (Asia) Private Limited, 1 New Industrial Road, Singapore 536196 • Marshall Cavendish International (Thailand) Co Ltd. 253 Asoke, 12th Flr, Sukhumvit 21 Road, Klongtoey Nua, Wattana, Bangkok 10110, Thailand • Marshall Cavendish (Malaysia) Sdn Bhd, Times Subang, Lot 46, Subang Hi-Tech Industrial Park, Batu Tiga, 40000 Shah Alam, Selangor Darul Ehsan, Malaysia

Marshall Cavendish is a trademark of Times Publishing Limited

All websites were available and accurate when this book was sent to press.

Library of Congress Cataloging-in-Publication Data

Bailer, Darice.
Donkeys / by Darice Bailer.
p. cm. — (Animals animals)
Includes index.
Summary: "Provides comprehensive information on the anatomy, special skills, habitats, and diet of donkeys"—Provided by publisher.
ISBN 978-0-7614-4875-4 (print)
ISBN 978-1-60870-617-4 (ebook)
1. Donkeys—Juvenile literature. I. Title.
SF361.B35 2012
636.1'82—dc22
2010033889
Photo research by Joan Meisel

Editor: Joy Bean
Publisher: Michelle Bisson
Art Director: Anahid Hamparian
Series Designer: Adam Mietlowski

Printed in Malaysia (T)
1 3 5 6 4 2

Contents

Man's Gentle Helper

A fuzzy gray donkey stands behind a white fence near the gate to his farm. The donkey sees a car and a horse trailer coming toward him and wants to say hello. Stretching out his head, the donkey opens his mouth and *brays* a loud *ee-aw*! The trailer drives past him, and the donkey canters behind it all the way to the stable. There the car stops, the rear door of the trailer opens, and a little brown horse walks slowly down a wooden ramp.

The *foal* misses his mother and is frightened on this strange farm. The donkey trots over and drapes his head over the foal's shoulder to comfort him. At night, when the little foal lies down on his new straw bed, the donkey snuggles next to him in the dark. He

In order to make itself known, a donkey will bray loudly to passers-by.

tucks the lonely foal at his side, keeping him warm as the foal falls fast asleep.

Donkeys are friendly and affectionate animals that look like small horses and belong to the same family as horses and zebras. Their genus, or group, name is *Equus*, which is Latin for *horse*. Donkeys, horses, and zebras come from the same prehistoric ancestors.

The donkey's scientific name is *Equus asinus*. Up until the late 1700s the donkey was called an ass. However, the word *ass* is not a very polite one, and people decided to call the animal by its color rather than its scientific name. *Dun* means grayish brown, and there is an Old English word *dunkey* that means a small, grayish brown animal.

The donkey is a *tame* animal, but its ancestors were wild. Donkeys are the *descendants* of the African wild ass, which lived more than 10,000 years ago and galloped across the hot deserts of northern Africa and Arabia. The animals looked like Arabian horses with striped legs. At first, early humans hunted the African wild ass for food and might have used its skin for clothing.

6

Donkeys have been helpful to humans for many centuries. This painting shows donkeys traveling with ancient Egyptians during the twelfth century BCE.

Early people drew pictures of African wild asses on the walls of their caves and learned that they could tame the animals to help them in many ways. So the African wild ass was domesticated about 5,000 or 6,000 years ago, and humans began using the tamed donkeys to ride, pull, and carry things for them. Before then, men and women had to carry everything they needed themselves. Now they had donkeys that were strong enough to help them and carry heavy loads on their backs.

Ancient Egyptians took advantage of these hardworking animals in farming, harnessing them to help to plant seeds and plow fields.

By 1000 BCE people often traveled on the backs of donkeys throughout Egypt and western Asia. Like

Species Chart

◆ *Equus asinus* is a tamed, or domesticated, donkey. Its ancestor is *Equus africanus*, the African wild ass. The African wild ass, which is only found in northeast Africa, is one of the world's rarest mammals and is nearly extinct. The animal is light gray, with long, slender legs, and it is graceful and fast. It weighs about 440 to 510 pounds (200 to 230 kg). The Somali wild ass, a subspecies, has a light, shiny coat and striped legs like a zebra's.

African wild asses, with their uniquely striped legs, are nearly extinct today.

trains and cars in the future, donkeys helped people travel and trade far away. King Ferdinand II of Spain gave Christopher Columbus six donkeys to load on his ship for his second voyage to the New World (1493–1496). The king might have worried how Columbus would get around or carry things once he reached shore.

Today there are about 44 million donkeys in the world, and they are found on every continent except Antarctica.

Donkeys come in many different sizes and colors. The most common color is gray, but they can also be brown, black, reddish brown, white, or spotted.

There are hundreds of different breeds of donkeys around the world, and some breeds are naturally larger than others. The American mammoth is the largest of four breeds found in North America, and the Mediterranean miniature is the smallest. Mammoths are more than 56 inches (1.4 m) tall, and miniatures are no taller than 36 inches (0.9 m). Miniatures make wonderful pets because they are one of the friendliest and most affectionate donkeys.

The United States has the largest population of *feral* donkeys. A Spanish explorer brought the first

donkeys to the American continent in 1598. Later, Western pioneers and gold miners traveled by donkey or packed their mining pans, picks, shovels, and strainers on the animals' back. Sometimes donkeys escaped from their owners to live in the wild. Thousands of feral donkeys, called *burros*, now live in the western United States.

Wild burros are found nuzzling on a beautiful day.

2 Desert Hardy and Friendly

Wild asses had features that helped them survive in hot and rocky deserts for thousands of years, and today's donkeys have some of those same features. Donkeys are intelligent animals that will refuse to do anything that is unsafe. People call their refusal stubbornness, but donkeys are usually trying to protect themselves.

Donkeys are friendly animals, and they like to be around other donkeys. They also enjoy being around ponies, sheep, goats, cows, chickens, cats, and dogs. They bond strongly with other animals, and if one of the animals a donkey lives with moves to a new home or dies, the donkey will pace, bray, and search for the missing animal.

Donkeys are friendly animals and like being around people and other animals.

Donkeys have excellent memories and remember someone who was kind to them. A donkey might lay its head on the shoulder of someone who is familiar to it. Donkeys make all sorts of noises when they are excited to see someone. They snort and snuffle at each other, especially when they are standing close to each other. When they bray, they stretch out their necks and heads and make a loud *hee-haw* sound. This comes from air being drawn into their lungs on the *hee* and being let out on the *haw*, and the noise can sound like a trumpet! Donkeys bray when they are happy or as a greeting. They also bray when they want to be fed or when they are frightened or lonely. Donkeys call out to one another across a field. They bray so loudly that they can be heard up to 2 miles (3.2 kilometers) away. Their ancestors needed loud voices to hear one another when they were spread out in the desert.

Donkeys, like their ancestors, try to protect the animals around them in their territory. Donkeys will watch over a flock of sheep or goats and guard them against *predators* such as foxes and coyotes. Today, farmers and ranchers are starting to keep donkeys to protect their sheep and lambs.

A donkey's ears are large in order to help the animal hear sounds from far away.

Like their wild ancestors, donkeys can see and hear very well to protect themselves from danger. Donkeys have large eyes that can spot animals moving in the distance. Their long ears act like radar and help them pick up sound so they can hear another animal far away. Their ears also have blood vessels just beneath the skin. Air flows around the donkey's ears and cools the donkey's blood, which helps the animal cool down.

Nonstop work in very hot weather is not good for donkeys, though. Their fur is usually light and shiny to reflect heat and help them stay cool. However, they need cover from the hot sun. Donkeys look like ponies, with their long ears and fluffy coats. Their coats can protect the animals from chill for a while but cannot keep them warm, so donkeys need to be covered with a blanket or rug when it is cold outside. Their coats are not waterproof, and donkeys need shelter from heavy rain. When donkeys get very cold or wet, they can catch pneumonia. Donkeys like to roll in the dirt because it feels good and coats their fur with dust to keep away insects. Donkeys also groom each other, nibbling each other's necks and *flanks*.

A donkey's mane is coarse and stiff. It is not as soft or thick as a horse's mane. The bristles are short, and they stand up straight instead of drape over the donkey's neck like a horse's mane. Most donkeys also have a dark stripe across their shoulders and down their backs. The hair on their tail hangs in a long *tassel*.

Donkeys cannot run very fast. They plod along and walk slowly, although they are remarkably

Most donkeys have a distinctive stripe across their shoulders.

Donkeys' teeth are made to help them tear and chew grass and other food.

sure-footed. Their hoofs are tough and sturdy, and donkeys can climb steep and rocky hills. Donkey hooves are made of the same tough protein as human fingernails. Like fingernails, their hooves keep growing, and donkeys need them trimmed every two months. Otherwise their hooves grow too long and curl up. Then donkeys are forced to walk on their heels, which is very painful for them.

Donkeys are *herbivores* and like to nibble on grass. When they graze, they tear off a blade of grass and grind it with their teeth. They get their adult teeth between the ages of four and five, and those teeth are large and strong. The top surfaces of their teeth are flat to help them tear and chew grass and tough plants that are found in the desert. Donkeys eat mostly grass, straw, and hay, and adults might go through about 10 to 13 pounds (4.5 to 6 kg) of hay or straw a day. Carrots are one of their favorite snacks.

Donkeys are able to absorb the water that is found in juicy plants, and that helps them go for a long time without drinking. Although donkeys may lose fluids in the heat, they can *hydrate* quickly once they are able to drink. Next to camels, donkeys are the most desert-hardy animals, and they can handle the heat and lack of food and water better than most large African mammals.

3 The Life Cycle of Donkeys

When donkeys are three or four years old, they are ready to have babies, or foals. A male donkey can mate with a female horse, or mare, and a female donkey, or jenny, can mate with a male horse, or stallion. A donkey can even mate with a zebra. After they mate, males and females usually do not stay together. The male leaves the female and she takes care of the foal by herself.

A jenny is pregnant for about a year. As she gets ready to give birth, a wild jenny will leave the other animals she lives with and go off on her own. Donkeys usually give birth to just one foal. Twins are rare because it is difficult for the jenny to carry both of them inside her. Most foals are born at night,

This female donkey is a good mother and companion for her growing foal.

between the hours of 11 p.m. and 3 a.m. In the wild, that is when most predators are asleep and cannot hurt the newborn.

When the foal is born, the jenny will lick her foal all over to clean it and dry it because it is important that her foal not catch cold. After the mother and foal rest, the jenny will reach over and give her baby a gentle nudge to its feet. Donkeys—and horses—do not nurse lying down like cats or dogs, and it is important that the foal stand up so it can nurse. Its mother's sweet milk is thick on the first day, and it is filled with nutrients to help the foal survive and protect it for life. Foals need to stand up and nurse from their mothers within a couple of hours after they are born. Because they have been developing for a year inside their mothers, foals are completely developed, so they can walk and trot on the first day.

At first foals struggle to their feet and are unsteady. They do not know how to use their new legs, and they might wobble and fall. It may take them three times before they are able to stand on their own. As the newborn nurses from its mother, a strong bond is

Did You Know . . .
When a male donkey and a female horse mate, their foal is called a *mule*. The foal born to a male horse and a female donkey is called a *hinny*. Mules have the body of horses and are very fast. They are also good, strong workers.

22

A mother donkey helps her newborn up to its feet for the first time.

formed. When the foal is full, it might trot out into the sunshine with its mother to explore the outside.

Like most babies, the little foal grows quickly. In two or three weeks, the foal begins eating grass and hay. It learns to drink fresh water by watching its mother, although it will continue nursing for a couple of months. When the foal is not eating, it might play with other foals, sheep, or goats that are around.

Galloping around in the sunshine helps a foal's bones grow stronger. A foal is playful and likes to crawl beneath its mother and come out the other side. Sometimes it wants to nurse when its mother is sleeping, and a foal may bite its mother's ear or lick its mother's face to wake her. Mothers stay near their foals for a few weeks and are never far away. If there are six or more females and their foals in a field, the mothers will take turns babysitting the young ones. The other mothers will go off and rest or eat grass.

Foals stop nursing when they are about four months old. A young male donkey is a called a *colt* until it turns three and becomes an adult. Then an adult male donkey is called a *jack*. A young female is called a *filly* until she is three. Then she is called a *jennet*, or jenny.

If donkeys are well cared for, they can live for more than fifty years. However, in poor countries, donkeys can die young when they are overworked, underfed, or unable to receive veterinarian care when they need it. The average donkey in Ethiopia only lives to be nine.

Two foals play with each other.

4 Donkey Rescue

Living in the United States, you will probably never see a donkey pulling a cart down your street. But in Africa, the Middle East, Asia, and South America, there are many poor villages that are not as modern as American cities and do not have roads that are paved for cars. A nine-year-old boy in Darfur (in the western region of the Sudan) may walk for hours in terrible heat to gather a jug of water for his family to drink. In Africa there are villages where donkeys with carts become moving vans to transport the family's carpets, dishes, pots, and pans to their next home. Donkeys and carts are also used as ambulances to take people to the hospital, which may be miles away. In Cairo, Egypt, and Mexico City, donkeys are used as

A donkey transports a number of baskets on its back for its owner.

garbage trucks. They carry carts filled with rubbish to the dump.

Donkeys are extremely important for a family's survival when they are all the family has for traveling or carrying things to and from home. They become the poor person's car or truck, hauling the family's oranges or mangoes to town so the produce can be sold in the market. In Africa, a family may depend on its donkey to bring water home for everyone to drink, including the family's cows, sheep, or goats. That can mean the difference between life and death, especially during long periods of dry weather, or *droughts*, when rivers or lakes might be miles away. Families also need help carrying heavy jars of water or stacks of firewood for cooking.

People know that they can train donkeys easily and that donkeys will work hard for them. They haul heavy jugs of water even when they are hungry, thirsty, or tired. Donkeys strain to pull carts stacked with dozens of heavy bricks. The donkeys work all day long, day after day. They may wear down and get sick, yet they trudge along as best as they can for their owners. The animals suffer quietly when someone beats them with a stick to go faster. Yet before

Donkeys are hardworking animals, such as this donkey pulling hay on a cart.

long the mistreated donkeys are too sick to work anymore. Their owners often do not have enough money to take care of them. It is cheaper for families to dump their donkeys by the side of the road rather than take them to the vet. They might tie their donkey to a tree and leave it there without any food or water. The donkey may starve to death.

Donkey sanctuaries allow donkeys to live their lives happily as they are well cared for and are not required to do any hard work.

A British woman named Dr. Elisabeth Svendsen had loved donkeys as a child and had always wanted to keep one. She bought her first donkey as a pet in 1968 and was horrified when she saw how badly others treated these sweet animals. Deciding to save as many donkeys as she could, Dr. Svendsen bought a farm and opened her first donkey *sanctuary* five years later. A sanctuary is a place where animals are protected from harm, and Dr. Svendsen wanted to dedicate her life to rescuing donkeys such as Hansel and Gretal. Hansel and Gretal were two donkeys she found that were starving and were so weak that they could not stand. Dr. Svendsen took care of them, and over the past forty years has rescued at least 14,000 more donkeys. The donkeys come mainly from Great Britain (England, Scotland, and Wales) and Northern Ireland. They may have been abused, or their owners might not have been able to care for them any longer. Dr. Svendsen has eight sanctuaries in England and one in Ireland. All together, her nine farms make up the largest sanctuary for

Did You Know . . .

When a child in Kenya has a bad cough, its mother will often give the child donkey's milk to drink. Donkey milk is very much like breast milk and is believed to protect a child from coughs and colds.

donkeys and mules in the world. Dr. Svendsen also has veterinarians who travel throughout the world caring for sick donkeys.

There are other donkey refuges in the world. In Israel, a woman named Lucy Fensom rescues donkeys that are caught in the fighting there. While you do not see many donkeys in modern Israel, they are very important in the lives of people who live in Arab or Israeli-Arab villages. A donkey from one orchard might be beaten for wandering into another's yard. Some people appear to frown upon donkeys and look down upon them, not only in the Middle East, but throughout the world. Fensom rescues the animals she finds and brings them to her farm, which she calls the Safe Haven for Donkeys in the Holy Land.

Fensom cares for 130 donkeys in Israel. The donkeys she brings back to the farm are treated with love and kindness. They can gallop on her sanctuary's grassy fields for the rest of their lives, and no one will hurt them ever again.

Three donkeys at a sanctuary in Spain take some time during the day to rest.

5 Donkeys and People

Even though people in modern countries do not need donkeys for work, donkeys can still be helpful in other ways. These gentle and friendly creatures are especially good with older people and children. The animals can help children, especially boys and girls with special needs.

At Spring Brook Farm in West Chester, Pennsylvania, children with disabilities have a chance to spend time with donkeys and other farm animals. The farm is built for children with handicaps. There are ramps for wheelchairs on the property, and children can roll their wheelchairs into the stable and reach up to pet one of the donkeys. A blind child can

Donkeys get along with people and enjoy getting attention from them.

rub his or her hands over the flank of a donkey and feel the shape of its body and the softness of its fur. All the animals are trained to be gentle with the children, and a donkey might sniff a carrot in a child's hands and then gently gobble it up. Children delight in petting and talking to the donkeys and hearing them snort and bray. Being around the sweet-natured donkeys helps children lose their fear of animals, get over their shyness, and laugh. Donkeys are known to bring a smile to a child's face.

Because donkeys have been shown to be helpful to children with disabilities, Dr. Svendsen started The Elisabeth Svendsen Trust for Children and Donkeys in England. There she has five special riding centers where children with autism or other special needs can pet and ride the animals. The children are given riding hats and are taken for rides around the school's fields and playgrounds. If a child is in a wheelchair or needs a walker to move around, he or she can get out of the wheelchair and up onto the donkey. Children have the opportunity to scratch the donkeys' ears and talk to them while they are riding them. Even children who are shy or anxious are often seen speaking to the animals and whispering in their ears. Children

Touching and riding a donkey is wonderful physical therapy for a teenager with disabilities.

with handicaps have the chance to make friends with donkeys. If a child was afraid of animals or of riding them, being in the saddle helps him or her overcome these fears. It is often the case that children look forward to seeing their new four-legged friends each week. Riding the animals helps strengthen children's leg muscles and improve their balance so they don't fall as much. Being around donkeys has been shown to boost children's self-confidence and bring joy and happiness to them.

Donkeys are eager to please and hungry for love. And, like a beloved dog, donkeys can be loyal and devoted pets. You can buy a donkey from the American Donkey and Mule Society, or you can buy donkeys from a breeder.

There are even donkeys you can adopt from the United States Bureau of Land Management (BLM) Wild Horse and Burro Adoption Program. In the Southwest there are about 3,800 wild burros living on public land. The animals are protected by the government. However, burros mate and multiply, and that means herds can double in size every four years. Donkeys do not

Miniature donkeys can make good pets if you have the space and time to care for them.

have any natural predators, so soon the animals crowd the land, eating all the grass and brush and fighting other wildlife for the little water there is to drink. That makes it difficult for other animals, such as desert tortoises, to survive. To solve the problem,

Donkeys are sometimes used by farmers to herd and guard their sheep.

the government is looking for people to adopt the burros, which can be easily tamed.

Donkeys and burros make great pets but need far more care than your average pet. They need to be fed and to have their stables cleaned each day. The donkeys need to be brushed and groomed, and their hooves have to be trimmed.

Donkeys are also much more expensive to feed and keep. They need a big stable or outdoor shelter where they can sleep and stay dry. They also need a large fenced-in yard that is at least 20 feet by 20 feet (6 m by 6 m)—which is probably bigger than your classroom at school. Donkeys need to be able to *graze* and run.

Donkeys make wonderful friends and companions. They have served humankind for thousands of years, helping people travel to faraway places and carry what they need with them. Donkeys still haul the most important things some families around the world need for survival. Donkeys have been devoted to men and women in ancient times and continue to help out today in modern times.

Glossary

bray—To make the loud *hee-haw* sound that a donkey makes, such as when it says hello.

burro—Another name for a small donkey. In Spanish, the word for donkey is *el burro*.

colt—A young male donkey, horse, or zebra.

descendants—Offspring, or the animals that come from previous generations.

domesticated—Made suitable for living and working with humans.

drought—A long period of very dry weather.

feral—Domesticated donkeys that returned to live in the wild.

flank—The side of an animal, between its ribs and hips.

foal—A young donkey, horse, or zebra. The word also means to give birth to a young donkey, horse, or zebra.

graze—To eat grass growing in a field.

herbivore—An animal that eats mainly plants.

hinny—The animal that is born to a female donkey and a stallion.

hydrate—To take in water and refill fluids.

jennet—The correct name for an adult female donkey. She is also called a jenny.

mascot—Something that is supposed to bring good luck and is kept as a symbol of an organization.

mule—The animal that is born to a male donkey and a female horse.

predator—An animal that hunts other animals for food.

sanctuary—A place where animals are safe and protected.

tame—Taken from the wild and taught to live with or help people.

tassel—A bunch of hairs or threads that are tied at one end and hang free.

Find Out More

Books

French, Jackie. *The Donkey Who Carried the Wounded: The Famous Story of Simpson and His Donkey—A True Anzac Legend*. Melbourne City: HarperCollins Publishers Australia, 2009.

Gallion, Anita. *Small-Scale Donkey Keeping*. Lexington, KY: Hobby Farms Press, 2010.

Palika, Liz. *Animals at Work* (ASPCA Kids). Hoboken, NJ: Howell Book House, 2009.

Stevenson, Robert Louis. *Travels with a Donkey*. New York: Atlas Pocket Classics, 2010.

Weaver, Sue. *The Donkey Companion: Selecting, Training, Breeding, Enjoying & Caring for Donkeys*. North Adams, MA: Storey Publishing, 2009.

Websites

The Barn at Spring Brook Farm
www.springbrook-farm.org

Creature Features: Donkeys
www.abc.net.au/creaturefeatures/facts/
donkeys.htm

The Donkey Sanctuary
www.thedonkeysanctuary.org.uk

Honolulu Zoo: Donkeys
www.honoluluzoo.org/donkey.htm

Safe Haven for Donkeys in the Holy Land
www.safehaven4donkeys.org

Index

Page numbers for illustrations are in **boldface**.

About the Author

Darice Bailer has written many books for Marshall Cavendish, including *Geese* and *Prairie Dogs* for the Animals Animals series and *How Do Caterpillars Become Butterflies?*, *Why Do Bears Hibernate?*, *How Do Tadpoles Become Frogs?*, and *Why Does it Thunder and Lightning?* for the Tell Me Why, Tell Me How series. A journalist for many years, Ms. Bailer has contributed to *The New York Times*, *The Washington Post*, and *The Hartford Courant*.